kripalu
seasonal
menus

fall and winter

from
Executive Chef
Deb Morgan

exploring the yoga of life.

Kripalu Center for Yoga & Health is a mission-driven, donor-supported 501(c)(3) nonprofit educational organization whose mission is to teach the art and science of yoga to produce thriving and health in individuals and society. The nation's most established center for yoga and holistic living, for 30 years Kripalu has been teaching people skills for optimal living through experiential education for the whole person: body, mind, and spirit.

For more information, go to kripalu.org or call 800.741.7353 to request a catalog or register for a program.
The word "Kripalu" is a registered trademark of Kripalu Center for Yoga & Health.

table of contents

lunches

dinners

seasonal specialties

introduction

The arrival of fall brings a fresh energy of excitement to the Kripalu Kitchen. With cooler temperatures also comes a bountiful array of fall vegetables—many from our local farm suppliers. This is the time for squash and potatoes, pumpkins and beets, carrots, parsnips, apples, and pomegranates, plus other nourishing cool-weather provisions.

For our winter recipe book, we've added to their natural amazingness by transforming these vegetables into mouth-watering dishes, including soups and stews, savory pies, lasagnas, casseroles, hearty entrées, roasted vegetables, and grain medleys. As with the first book in our series, we've arranged our recipes into meals just like we serve in our dining room. This gives you, the home cook, an idea of nutritionally sound and flavor-filled combinations. And as many meals feature a poultry or fish option in addition to the vegetarian version, our hope is that you find just the right balance in your menu planning. Feel free to get creative and mix and match different entrées and sides—or add in one of our delicious soups.

Just as Kripalu Yoga is more than a series of postures, the Kripalu cuisine is more than a collection of recipes. I hope you are inspired as much as I am by the Healthy Living notes that are sprinkled throughout this book. From Kathie Madonna Swift, one of our nutritionists, you'll learn a new term, "cephalic digestion"; I was thrilled that there is an actual term for what I feel is one of the prime components of health. Writer, poet, and yoga instructor Grace Jull also inspires us with a reminder about the importance of pleasure and gratitude. John Bagnulo's nutritional wisdom makes eating all these winter vegetables even more appealing! And Myron Katz, one of our steward supervisors, really inspires us with a new way to look at a dirty dish!

All in all, my hope is that this recipe book, and all of Kripalu's educational resources, keep you curious and engaged in the pleasures of cooking and the joy of sharing the meals you create.

Feel free to contact me to share your stories of loving the world through food, and I hope to see you at Kripalu in the near future.

Cook love, live love,

Deb Morgan

acknowledgments

A heart-filled thank you and deep appreciation goes to the 70 individuals who comprise the Kripalu Kitchen team. The spirit with which you do each aspect of our work is truly the art of meditation in motion; my immense awe and gratitude for who you are and what you do.

Special appreciation goes to this season's chief recipe tester, Michael Pigott, who has been an invaluable member of our team for more than eight years. Deep gratitude to Jeremy Smith for being our excellent chef de cuisine, heartful manager, and dear comrade on this mission to bring the yoga of cooking to life in our kitchen.

Once again, I am blessed to work with the most outrageously dedicated marketing team on the planet, led in this project by Elena Erber and assisted by the talented wordsmith Grace Welker, with precision editing by Ashley Winseck and the expert coordination of Joyce Monaco.

The beautiful photography in our pages is courtesy of the much-appreciated talent of Jennifer May. And again, I owe a sincere thank you to Jessica Bard for her food styling expertise and ability to make these recipes come to life.

stocking your pantry

Any chef will tell you that the three keys to success in the kitchen are prep, prep, and prep. As with many aspects of life, a satisfying kitchen experience can be enhanced with a little time put into preparation.

First, the menu. A little planning goes a long way and can save both time and money as you buy foods for specific meals and create a coordinated effort to use leftovers. Second, your pantry. Creating a pantry gives you the ease of knowing that items used again and again are readily available. With a well-stocked pantry, more of your energy will be free to cook and create meals that nourish you and your family. Enjoy!

To help you along the way, I offer here a list of nonperishable items found in this book.

oils and vinegars
apple cider vinegar
balsamic vinegar
extra-virgin olive oil
grape seed oil
safflower oil
toasted sesame oil

nuts, seeds, and dry fruit
almonds
blueberries
cashews
cranberries
currants
dates
hazelnuts
pecans
pumpkin seeds
raisins
walnuts

dry herbs, spices, and seasonings
allspice
basil
black pepper
cayenne
chili powder
cinnamon
coriander
cumin
curry
dill
fennel seed
garam masala
garlic
ginger
mustard seeds
nutmeg
nutritional yeast
oregano
paprika
rosemary
saffron
sage
sea salt
tamari
tarragon
thyme
turmeric
zahtar

pasta
elbows
lasagna
spaghetti

beans (canned or dry)
chickpeas
kidney
navy
pinto
red and green lentils

grains
barley
basmati rice
brown rice
millet
quinoa
wheat berries

flours
all-purpose flour
baking soda and powder
cornmeal
pastry flour
rice flour

canned tomatos
crushed
diced
paste

sweeteners
honey
maple syrup
molasses
sugar (organic)

specialty items
capers
chipotles
coconut milk
Earth Balance™
filo dough
kombu
lime and lemon juices
mustard
olives
pomegranate
soy milk
sun-dried tomatoes
tamarind paste
white wine
Worcestershire sauce

lunches

lunch savory-style pies

Grecian Pie ▪ Tofu Almond Pie ▪ Roasted Vegetables with Dates ▪ Cucumber Tomato Salad

There is something about the combination of flavors and textures in these filo pies that makes it virtually impossible to choose a favorite—try them both and see for yourself! On the side, dates add a surprising sweetness to roasted vegetables—a cold-weather favorite. To top off the meal, we add a crispy cucumber tomato salad served with a tangy yogurt dressing.

grecian pie

Makes one 9x13-inch pie

2 medium sweet potatoes, peeled and sliced
2 medium potatoes, peeled and sliced
3 tablespoons extra-virgin olive oil
1 red onion, sliced
1/2 cup sun-dried tomatoes, soaked and sliced
2 tablespoons chopped garlic
1 teaspoon dried thyme
1 teaspoon dried fennel seed
1 teaspoon sea salt
Pinch of black pepper
2 tablespoons white wine
1 cup fresh goat cheese, crumbled
1/2 cup sliced Kalamata olives
14 sheets filo dough, thawed overnight in the refrigerator*
3/4 cup butter or Earth Balance™ (vegan spread, melted)

* Filo (also known as phyllo) is a delicate sheet of dry but pliable pastry that is very sensitive to moisture. It is purchased frozen and must be thawed completely before use. To prevent it from becoming sticky, it is best to defrost it slowly in the refrigerator overnight. Keep covered with a dry cloth while working with it. Look for packages of filo pastry that are conveniently wrapped in 2 separate pouches—in case you only need about half for a recipe!

Steam the sweet potatoes and potatoes separately until tender but not mushy, about 10 minutes each. Set aside.

Heat the oil in a sauté pan over medium heat. Add the onion, sun-dried tomatoes, and garlic and sauté until onion starts to brown. Add the thyme and fennel seed and sauté for a few more minutes. Add the salt, pepper, and wine and stir to loosen any browned bits from bottom of pan. Sauté a few more minutes and set aside. Once cooled, fold in goat cheese and olives.

Unwrap filo dough and cover it with a dry cloth to prevent it from drying out. Use a pastry brush to coat the bottom of a 9x13-inch baking dish with a little of the melted butter. Layer in 7 sheets of filo, brushing a little butter between each layer. (It's okay if the filo bends up the sides of the pan a little bit)

Top the filo layers with the sliced potatoes and then the onion mixture. Then top with the sliced sweet potatoes. Top with another 7 layers of filo, brushing a little butter between each one and a little on the top.

Bake in a 375-degree oven until the filo is golden brown and crispy, about 45 minutes.

tofu almond pie

Makes one 9x13-inch pie

3 tablespoons extra-virgin olive oil
1 yellow onion, diced
4 stalks celery, chopped
2 carrots, small diced
2 teaspoons dried thyme
2 teaspoons dried sage
1 teaspoon salt
Pinch of black pepper
1/2 teaspoon fennel seed
1 teaspoon dried dill
2 tablespoons white wine
1 1/2 pounds firm tofu, cut into small cubes
1/4 cup wheat-free tamari
1/4 cup chopped parsley
1 cup chopped, toasted almonds
21 sheets filo dough (about half a package),
    thawed overnight in the refrigerator
1/2 cup Earth Balance™ (vegan spread), melted

Heat the oil in a sauté pan over medium heat. Add the onion, celery, and carrots and sauté until onion starts to brown. Add the thyme and sage and sauté for a few more minutes. Add the salt, pepper, and wine and stir to loosen any browned bits from bottom of pan. Add the tofu and tamari and sauté gently for 5 minutes. Remove from heat and stir in the parsley and almonds. Set aside.

Unwrap filo dough and cover it with a dry cloth to prevent it from drying out. Use a pastry brush to coat the bottom of a 9x13-inch baking dish with a little of the melted Earth Balance. Layer in 7 sheets of filo, brushing a little melted Earth Balance between each layer.

Spread half of the tofu-vegetable mixture over the filo. Layer in another 7 layers of filo, brushing a little melted Earth Balance between each layer. Add the remaining tofu-vegetable mixture. Top with a final 7 layers of filo dough, brushing a little melted Earth Balance between each layer and on top.

Bake in a 375-degree oven until the filo is golden brown and crispy, 35 to 45 minutes.

roasted vegetables with dates

Serves 4

1 small carrot, cut into 1/2-inch x 2-inch sticks
1 small beet, cut into 1/2-inch x 2-inch sticks
1 small onion, sliced
1/2 red bell pepper, sliced
1 1/2 tablespoons extra-virgin olive oil
Pinch of salt
1/4 cup pitted dates, sliced

Preheat oven to 400 degrees. Combine the ingredients in large bowl and toss well. Place in a large baking pan and cover with foil. Bake until vegetables are tender, 30 to 40 minutes. Gently toss the vegetables together and transfer to a serving dish. Serve hot.

cucumber tomato salad

Serves 4

for the dressing
1 cup plain yogurt
2 1/2 tablespoons fresh lemon juice
1 tablespoon chopped garlic
1/4 teaspoon sea salt
1 teaspoon extra-virgin olive oil

for the salad
1 English cucumber, peeled and diced
1 1/2 cups grape tomatoes
3 cups chopped, well-rinsed romaine lettuce
1 cup fresh chopped cilantro
1/4 cup fresh chopped mint

Combine the dressing ingredients in a bowl and whisk until well combined.

Toss together the salad ingredients in a large bowl. Serve the dressing on the side or add to the salad before serving.

healthy living notes
harvest nutrition
John Bagnulo, PhD, nutritionist

Although most of the fruits and vegetables we associate with autumn are not related botanically, they offer our bodies a consistent nutritional theme. Apples, pears, grapes, beets, and squash are all excellent sources of soluble fiber and all but the squash are great sources of one particular type of soluble fiber: pectin. Pectin has a long list of research-substantiated health effects that range from lowering cholesterol levels to removing heavy metals and other contaminants from the body. This is truly nature's soft detox agent and a great way to prepare for the short days of winter.

In addition to this great source of soluble fiber, these fruits and vegetables are very alkalizing as they are all great sources of potassium. They have unique phytonutrients that are protective against carcinogens. The ellagic acid in grapes and the betacyanin in beets stand out in this area, but winter squash varieties that cook to a dark orange are loaded with a wide variety of carotenoids that offer similar protection. Autumn makes it easy to eat the amount of fruits and vegetables that we need to feel our best.

lunch indian inspiration

Indian Chickpeas • Vegetable Biryani • Potato Samosa • Tamarind Sauce • Cilantro Mint Chutney

We serve our Indian chickpeas two ways, with heavy cream and vegan-style with coconut milk. In both versions, the spices come to life in a pool of delicious sauce. Serve over our Biryani with a side of Potato Samosa topped with tamarind sauce or cilantro mint chutney.

indian chickpeas

Serves 4

2 cups cooked or canned chickpeas
1 tablespoon ghee or vegetable oil
1/2 Spanish onion, diced
1 1/2 teaspoons minced garlic
1 1/2 teaspoons minced ginger
1 1/2 teaspoons coriander
1 1/2 teaspoons cumin
1 1/2 teaspoons garam masala— *1 pt cumin*
1 1/2 teaspoons chili powder *1/4 pt allspice*
2 cups crushed tomatoes
1/2 teaspoon sea salt
1 1/2 cups heavy cream or 1 cup coconut milk
2 tablespoons chopped fresh cilantro

Heat the ghee or oil in a sauté pan over medium-high heat. Add the onions, garlic, and ginger and sauté until softened, 5 to 8 minutes. Add the spices and sauté for 1 minute. Reduce the heat to medium-low. Add tomatoes and salt and simmer gently for 30 minutes.

Use an immersion blender to puree the mixture right in the pot or transfer it to a blender and puree until smooth. (Use caution while pureeing hot liquid; keep blades of an immersion blender submerged and if using a blender, work in batches, filling the blender jar only halfway and hold a cloth over the lid while pureeing.) Return the puree to the pan and add the chickpeas and heavy cream or coconut milk. Over medium heat, simmer until heated through, 5 to 8 minutes. Garnish with cilantro.

vegetable biryani

Serves 4

1 1/2 cups white basmati rice
2 1/2 cups water
1 teaspoon sea salt
Pinch of saffron threads
2 tablespoons ghee or vegetable oil
1/2 small onion, medium diced
1 tablespoon minced ginger
1 tablespoon chopped garlic
1 teaspoon turmeric
1 small carrot, small diced
3/4 cup frozen peas
1/2 cup raisins
1/2 cup whole cashews
Fresh chopped cilantro (optional)

Rinse and drain the rice. Combine the rice, water, salt, and saffron in a 4 or 5 quart pot with a fitted lid. Bring to a boil. Reduce heat to low, cover and cook until rice is tender, 12 to 15 minutes. Turn off heat and let stand, covered, for a few minutes before fluffing with a fork.

Heat the ghee or oil in a sauté pan over medium-high heat. Add the onions, ginger, and garlic and sauté until softened, 5 to 8 minutes. Add the turmeric and carrots and sauté for 5 more minutes. Remove from heat, add peas and raisins, and set aside.

Uncover the rice and fluff gently with a fork. Add the carrot mixture and cashews, and gently combine. Garnish with fresh cilantro, if desired.

potato samosa

Makes 4–6

2 tablespoons Earth Balance™ (vegan spread) or
  ghee
1 small onion, medium diced
1/2 teaspoon fennel seed
1 teaspoon cumin seed
2 large boiling potatoes, peeled and diced
2 teaspoons white wine
1/4 teaspoon sea salt
1 teaspoon fresh thyme leaves
Pinch of black pepper
1 recipe Turnover (Empanada) Dough

Heat the Earth Balance or ghee in a large sauté
pan over medium-high heat. Add the onions and
cook, stirring often until they are lightly browned,
about 8 minutes. Add the fennel and cumin seeds
and sauté for 1 minute. Add the potatoes, wine,
and salt and cook the potatoes until soft, about 12
to 15 minutes, stirring often.

Stir in the thyme and pepper. Use a potato masher
(or tines of a large fork) to lightly mash the
potatoes, keeping about half intact. Cool and use
as filling for Turnover (Empanada) Dough (recipe
follows).

turnover (empanada) dough

Makes 6–7

1 1/2 cups unbleached all-purpose flour
1 1/2 cups whole wheat flour
1 1/2 teaspoons sea salt
1 1/2 cups non-hydrogenated palm shortening
1/2 cup cold water

In a mixing bowl, combine the flours and salt. Mix
in the shortening with a fork until well combined
and crumbly. Add water slowly, mixing until just
combined.

On a lightly floured work surface, roll out the
dough fairly thin, about 1/8-inch thick. Cut into
6 or 7 6-inch circles. (You may need to roll out
scraps of dough to get final circles.)

Place 1/3 cup of filling on one side of each dough
circle and fold over. Pinch or crimp the edges to
seal. Bake at 425 degrees until crust is golden and
flaky, 15 to 20 minutes. Serve samosas hot with the
Tamarind Sauce and the Cilantro Mint Chutney.

tamarind sauce

Makes about 1 cup

1 teaspoon sunflower oil
1/2 teaspoon cumin seeds
Pinch of chili flakes
3 tablespoons tamarind paste
1/2 cup Rapadura™ organic whole cane sugar (or
  other sugar)
1/3 cup plus 1 tablespoon water
1/8 teaspoon sea salt

Heat the oil in a sauté pan over medium heat.
Add the cumin and chili flakes and sauté for 30
seconds, being careful not to burn the spices.
Stir in the tamarind paste, sugar, water, and salt.
Simmer gently until the sauce becomes thick but
remains pourable, about 15 minutes. Cool. Serve
with samosas.

cilantro mint chutney

Makes 1 1/2 cups

1 bunch cilantro, well-rinsed and chopped
1/4 cup chopped fresh mint
2 tablespoons diced red onion
1/4 jalapeño, chopped
3 tablespoons extra-virgin olive oil
1 tablespoon minced ginger
2 tablespoons fresh lemon juice
1/4 teaspoon salt
1/4 teaspoon ground corriander
1/4 teaspoon garam marsala
2 tablespoons honey

Combine all ingredients in a food processor and
pulse to combine until coarsely chopped. Serve
with samosas.

facing the dishes
Myron Katz, Kripalu Steward Supervisor

We all have situations in our lives that may appear overwhelming, times when an inner voice tells us "this just can't be done" or "this is too much." In the Kripalu dishroom, the possibility exists for that to become an ongoing universal chant! Imagine how daunting it is to have—in a very short period of time—hundreds of dishes circling round in front of you, all calling out "scrape me, sort me, spray me, and wash me."

In moments of potential frustration or overwhelm, as the trays keep coming toward me, the first thing I do is take a deep breath and consciously allow my focus to rest on the one tray of dishes that is in front of me. This makes me feel immediately calm, and I begin to tap into an energy source that was not accessible when I was feeling frustrated. As the rush of dishes continues toward me, what I perceived as overwhelming just moments before starts to become playful and engaging, an invigorating game almost.

Over time I have learned how to apply this practice of presence in the midst of any seemingly chaotic situation. I've found that there always exists an opening to the core of my being. And that this opening connects me with a place of inner stillness—so that no matter how challenging something is, I can be in joy, in peacefulness, in loving-kindness, and enjoy the adventurous journey of living and working. This is true in the Kripalu dishroom, washing thousands of dishes each day, and at home in my own kitchen, facing one pot.

Three Sisters Casserole with Corn Bread Topping • Kale with Pepitas

In honor of what is traditionally known by Native Americans as the three sisters—corn, beans, and squash—we developed this simple, great tasting casserole. Some kale topped with crunchy pepitas (pumpkin seeds) make this nutritious vegan meal complete.

three sisters casserole with corn bread topping

Makes one 9x13-inch casserole

filling
2 tablespoons Earth Balance™ (vegan spread)
1 cup chopped onion
3 stalks celery, chopped
1 tablespoon minced garlic
1 1/2 teaspoons ground coriander
1 1/2 teaspoons cumin
4 cups butternut squash, peeled and cut
    into cubes
2 cups canned diced tomatoes
1 teaspoon sea salt
1/2 cup water or vegetable stock
1 3/4 cups cooked pinto beans, drained
1 cup frozen corn

corn bread topping
1 1/4 cups fine cornmeal
1/2 cup whole wheat pastry flour
1/2 cup unbleached all-purpose flour
1 tablespoon baking powder
1/4 teaspoon sea salt
1/4 cup water
3/4 cup soy milk
2 tablespoons sunflower oil
1/3 cup maple syrup
1/4 teaspoon vanilla extract

make the filling:
Heat Earth Balance in a large saucepan over medium-high heat. Add the onion and sauté until it starts to brown, about 8 minutes. Add the celery and sauté until just tender. Stir in the garlic, coriander, and cumin and sauté for 1 minute. Add the squash, tomatoes, and salt and cook 5 minutes, stirring occasionally. Stir in 1/2 cup water or stock and bring to a boil. Reduce heat to medium-low and simmer, partially covered, until squash is tender, 10 to 15 minutes. Turn off heat and stir in the beans and corn. Transfer to a 9x13-inch casserole pan and set aside.

make the corn bread topping:
Combine cornmeal, flours, baking powder, and salt in a large bowl. Combine water, soy milk, sunflower oil, maple syrup, and vanilla extract in another bowl and mix well. Add the wet ingredients to the dry mixture and stir until everything is just blended. The batter will be thick.

to assemble and bake:
Spread the corn bread batter over the vegetable filling evenly all the way to the edges. Bake in a 375-degree oven until corn bread is cooked through and filling is heated through and the top is slightly browned, 25 to 30 minutes.

kale with pepitas

Serves 4

1/2 cup pepitas
6 cups chopped, well-rinsed, Lacinato kale
Extra-virgin olive oil (optional)

Place pepitas in a small dry skillet over medium heat. Stir continuously until they begin to pop and darken slightly. Remove from heat and set aside.

Combine the kale with 1/2 cup of water in a large sauté pan. Place over high heat and bring to a boil. Reduce heat to low, cover, and simmer gently until water is evaporated and kale is tender. To serve, add a splash of olive oil, if desired, and toss with pepitas.

lunch a thanksgiving twist

Sage Turkey Burgers • **Vegan Black Bean Burgers** • **Yam Fries** • **Cranberry Relish**
• **Corn Chowder**

*For this time of year, I couldn't resist the traditional flavors of the season. Serve your Sage
Turkey Burger or Vegan Black Bean Burger on a yummy bun (we use our brioche buns)
topped with the cranberry relish with sides of yam fries and corn chowder. Pure happiness.*

sage turkey burgers

Makes 4 quarter-pound burgers

1 pound ground turkey meat
1/2 teaspoon sea salt
Pinch of black pepper
2 tablespoons chopped fresh sage
1 tablespoon extra-virgin olive oil
1 1/2 teaspoons chopped thyme leaves
2 teaspoons Worcestershire sauce

Combine all ingredients in a bowl and mix well.

Divide the mixture into 4 and shape into burger
patties.

Grill or bake the burgers at 350 degrees until
cooked through, 15 to 20 minutes. (The burgers
should reach an internal temperature of
165 degrees.)

Serve the burgers on buns or alone with toppings
of your choice.

vegan black bean burgers

Makes 4 large burgers

1 cup toasted pepitas (pumpkin seeds)
1 cup pecan meal, or 1 1/4 cups raw pecans
2 1/2 cups cooked black beans, drained well
1 cup cooked brown rice
2 tablespoons extra-virgin olive oil
1 small Spanish onion, diced

1 tablespoon chopped garlic
1 tablespoon cumin
1 1/2 teaspoons ground coriander
1 1/2 teaspoons dried sage
1 teaspoon dried thyme
1 teaspoon sea salt
Pinch of black pepper

Place the pumpkin seeds in the bowl of a food
processor and pulse a few times to partially grind
the seeds. If using whole pecans, place them in
the processor and pulse to create a pecan meal.
Add half the black beans and 3/4 of the rice and
pulse to lightly mash. Transfer to a large bowl.

In a sauté pan, heat the olive oil and sauté the
onion and garlic for a few minutes. Add the cumin
and coriander and sauté 1 minute. Stir in the sage,
thyme, salt, and pepper. Add this mixture to the
mashed bean mixture along with the remaining
beans and rice. Mix everything together well.

Divide the mixture into 4 (or more if you'd like
smaller burgers) and shape into patties. Grill or
bake at 350 degrees for 15 to 20 minutes. Let
stand for 5 minutes before serving. (This allows
the burger to firm up.)

Serve the burgers on buns or alone with toppings
of your choice.

yam fries

Serves 4

2 yams or sweet potatoes
2 tablespoons extra-virgin olive oil
Pinch of sea salt
Pinch of black pepper
Pinch of chili powder
Pinch of cayenne pepper

Preheat oven to 375 degrees. Cut each potato lengthwise into 8 wedges, or more if yams are very large. Transfer to a large bowl and add the oil and spices. Toss well until potatoes are coated with the spice mixture.

Place the potato wedges on a large baking sheet. Bake until yams are tender on the inside and browned on the outside, about 30 minutes.

cranberry relish

Makes 1 1/4 cups

1 cup frozen cranberries
1/2 teaspoon orange zest
3/4 cup apple cider
1 teaspoon fresh lemon juice
1 teaspoon fresh orange juice
Pinch of sea salt
2 tablespoons honey

Heat cranberries, zest, cider, and juices in a sauce pot over medium heat. Add salt and simmer gently until the cranberries plump and the liquid is reduced, about 20 minutes.

Mash the berries with a spoon against the side of the pot until most are broken up. Stir in the honey. Transfer to a serving bowl and refrigerate until cool. Serve chilled.

corn chowder

Serves 4

2 tablespoons Earth Balance™ (vegan spread) or
    butter
1/4 teaspoon cumin
Pinch of paprika
1 small onion, diced
3 stalks celery, diced
1 leek, sliced
2 cups peeled, diced potatoes
3 cups fresh or frozen corn kernels
3 cups water or vegetable stock
1 teaspoon salt
1 cup heavy cream or nondairy milk of choice
Pinch of nutmeg
Black pepper, to taste

In a large soup pot, heat the Earth Balance or butter over medium heat. Add the cumin and paprika and heat for 30 seconds. Add the onion, celery, and leek and sauté until tender.

Increase the heat to high and add the potatoes, corn, and water or stock. Bring to a boil and add the salt. Reduce heat to low and gently simmer until potatoes are tender, about 15 minutes.

Transfer half the soup to a blender and puree until smooth. Return the puree to the rest of the soup and add the cream or milk, nutmeg, and pepper. Simmer gently until heated through. Serve hot.

lunch exotic essentials

Chicken or Tofu Curry Stew ▪ Fried Rice ▪ Exotic Carrot Salad

This is one of those wonderful meals that can be pulled together from leftovers yet will always taste new and different. Try our vegetarian version with tofu or start with fresh or cooked chicken, which naturally lends itself to a succulent stew. The next time you cook rice, make some extra so the fried rice becomes a quick and easy add-on—or a meal unto itself. The Exotic Carrot Salad is so yummy, expect it to become a family favorite!

chicken or tofu curry stew

Serves 4 or more

1/2 cup unbleached all-purpose flour
4 tablespoons butter or safflower oil
1 medium onion, diced
1/2 cup diced celery
1/3 cup diced apple
1 1/2 teaspoons curry powder
1 teaspoon turmeric
Pinch of cayenne pepper
2 teaspoons sea salt
6 cups chicken or vegetable stock
3 cups cooked chicken meat, pulled or cubed
or 1 pound tofu cut into cubes
1 tablespoon agave syrup or honey

Make a roux by heating 3 tablespoons of the butter or oil in a large, heavy-bottomed soup pot over medium-low heat. Whisk in the flour and stir constantly until the roux is heated through without taking on color, about 2 minutes. Transfer the roux to a bowl and set aside.

In the same pot, heat the remaining tablespoon of the butter or oil over medium heat. Add the onion and celery and sauté until they are softened and somewhat translucent. Add the apple, spices, and salt and continue to sauté until apples just begin to soften.

Add the reserved roux and stir to combine. Slowly add the stock, whisking vigorously to prevent lumps. Add the chicken or tofu and simmer gently for 15 minutes. The stew will thicken. Stir in the agave syrup or honey. Taste and adjust the seasoning as desired.

Note If you prefer to make this recipe more soup-like, simply decrease the amount of roux that is used.

fried rice

Serves 4

for the sauce

1 tablespoon wheat-free tamari
1/2 teaspoon toasted sesame oil
1 tablespoon white wine

for the garnish (optional)

2 eggs, cracked and scrambled with a fork
1 tablespoon sesame oil for the eggs

for the rice

2 tablespoons sesame oil
4 cups cooked long grain brown rice
   or basmati rice
1 tablespoon minced ginger
1 tablespoon chopped garlic
2 trimmed scallions, sliced
1 small carrot, small diced
1 small Spanish onion, diced
1 cup frozen peas

make the sauce:

Combine the tamari, toasted sesame oil, and wine
in a small bowl. Set aside.

make the garnish (if using):

In a small pan, heat the sesame oil over medium
heat. Add the scrambled egg and let set without
stirring. Loosen the edges and flip over to set the
other side. Transfer to a cutting board and allow to
cool. Cut egg into small pieces and set aside.

to finish:

Heat the sesame oil in a large sauté pan, wok, or
a flat grill over high heat. Add the ginger, garlic,
scallions, carrot, and onion. Stir-fry for one minute
and then add the rice. Continue to stir-fry until
vegetables are just tender and the rice starts to
become toasted. Stir in the sauce mixture, frozen
peas, and egg until heated through.

exotic carrot salad

Makes about 4 cups

for the dressing

1/2 cup Veganaise ™ (egg-less mayonnaise)
1 tablespoon fresh lime juice
1 tablespoon honey
1 teaspoon grated ginger
2 tablespoons chopped fresh cilantro

for the salad

3 cups grated carrot
1/2 cup toasted, unsweetened shredded coconut
1/2 cup toasted, slivered almonds
1/3 cup dried cranberries

Whisk together the dressing ingredients in a large
mixing bowl. Add the salad ingredients and toss
together until thoroughly mixed. Serve at room
temperature or chilled.

lunch home-style comfort

Broccoli and Cheddar Quiche with Quinoa Crust • Roasted Red Potatoes • Home-Style Baked Beans

I love this version of quiche. Not only is it simple but because it utilizes quinoa instead of wheat, it is gluten-free as well. The quinoa magically sinks to the bottom of the dish to create a thin crust. Serve with roasted red potatoes and these comfort-food-style baked beans and you'll have the energy to split 10 cords of wood on a cold winter's day.

broccoli and cheddar quiche with quinoa crust

Makes one 9x13-inch quiche; serves 6–9

1/2 cup quinoa
2 tablespoons extra-virgin olive oil
1 Spanish onion, diced
1 tablespoon chopped garlic
4 cups medium-sized broccoli florets
12 eggs
2 cups whole milk
2 tablespoons fresh thyme leaves
1/2 teaspoon sea salt
Pinch of black pepper
1 cup grated cheddar cheese
1/4 cup grated Parmesan cheese

Rinse the quinoa well and set aside to drain.

Heat the olive oil in a sauté pan over medium heat. Add the onion and garlic and sauté until onion begins to brown, about 8 minutes. Add the broccoli and sauté for 1 minute, then turn off heat. Broccoli should still be crunchy. Cool slightly. Transfer the mixture to a lightly oiled 9x13-inch casserole dish and spread out evenly.

Sprinkle the cheddar cheese evenly over the vegetable mixture.

Combine the eggs, milk, thyme, salt, pepper, and rinsed quinoa in a large bowl and whisk until thoroughly combined. Pour immediately over the cheese-topped vegetable mixture.

Bake casserole in a 350-degree oven until cooked through and the top is just starting to brown, about 40 minutes. Remove the casserole from the oven and sprinkle the Parmesan cheese over the top. Return the casserole to the oven and bake until the Parmesan cheese is melted and just starting to brown, about 5 more minutes.

Let the casserole sit at least 10 minutes before serving.

roasted red potatoes

Serves 4

4 large or 8 small red potatoes, halved or
    quartered
1 tablespoon extra-virgin olive oil
3/4 teaspoon dried rosemary, broken up
1/4 teaspoon sea salt
Pinch of black pepper

Combine the ingredients in a large bowl and
toss well. Transfer to a baking sheet. Roast in a
425-degree oven until golden brown and slightly
crispy on the outside, about 30 minutes. Serve
hot.

home-style baked beans

Serves 4

2 3/4 cups canned navy beans (drained, liquid
    reserved) or 1 cup dry navy beans
1 1/2 tablespoons extra-virgin olive oil
1 small Spanish onion, chopped
1 1/2 tablespoons minced garlic
4 slices turkey bacon, minced (optional)
1 teaspoon chili powder
1/2 teaspoon onion powder
3 tablespoons tomato paste
3 tablespoons molasses
1 1/2 tablespoons stone-ground mustard
1/2 cup water (or bean-cooking water)
1 teaspoon sea salt
1/2 teaspoon dried thyme

If using the dry navy beans, rinse well and place
in a large bowl. Cover with water by 2 inches and
soak overnight. Drain the beans and place in a
pot with 4 cups fresh water and a 1-inch piece of
kombu. Bring to a boil, reduce heat and simmer
until beans are cooked through but still hold-
ing their shape. Add a pinch of salt at the end of
cooking. Drain the beans reserving the liquid and
set both aside.

Heat the oil in a large pot over medium-high heat.
Add the onion and garlic and sauté until onion
begin to brown. Add the bacon (if using), and
continue to sauté a few more minutes. Add the
chili powder, onion powder, and tomato paste and
sauté for 1 minute. Stir in the molasses, mustard,
water or reserved bean-cooking water, salt and
thyme and simmer for a few minutes. Add the
beans and gently stir to combine.

Transfer beans into baking dish, cover with a lid
or foil and bake at 350 degrees for 30 minutes
to heat through and allow sauce to thicken. Serve
hot.

healthy living notes
food and mood
Kathie Madonna Swift, MS, RD, nutritionist

Did you know that your brain is a reflection of the nutrients it receives from the biochemical information (food) you feed it? Your brain needs nourishment and whether you are upbeat or feeling blue is strongly influenced by how your "second brain" (your digestive tract) digests and absorbs the "information" you are eating. Thus, your mood is a mirror not only of what you eat but also how you digest!

Here are a few quick nutrition tips to boost your mood and lift your spirit:

1. Nourish your "mood-cell membranes" with healthy fats such as avocado, wild fatty fish (sardines, wild salmon, or black cod), nuts, seeds, olives, coconut, and smart oils like extra-virgin olive oil.

2. "B-happy" by including whole foods such as beans, dark, leafy green vegetables, and whole grains rich in B-vitamins in your diet.

3. Color your plate with vegetables, fruits, herbs, and spices that deliver a portfolio of antioxidants and anti-inflammatory jewels that keep cells healthy so that positive information can be transmitted without interference from cellular debris.

4. Capitalize on cephalic digestion, which means obtaining maximum nutrition from your meals and snacks by savoring the aesthetic qualities of your food, eating with awareness, and thoroughly chewing every bite.

5. Let the sunshine in—and on—you! Incidental sunlight helps your body manufacture vitamin D, which is vitally important for mood, mind, and memory.

lunch a taste of greece

Spinach Feta Casserole • Baked Winter Squash with Honey Walnuts • Red Lentil Soup

Though I love traditional spanakopita, our Spinach Feta Casserole provides the same great combination of flavors in a simpler format. Experiment with the squash recipe—it works wonderfully with a variety of squashes, including butternut, buttercup, kabocha, and delicata. The Red Lentil Soup is incredibly satisfying so be sure to make extra for the next day.

spinach feta casserole

Makes one 9x13-inch casserole dish

1 cup basmati rice
1/2 cup currants
2 tablespoons extra-virgin olive oil
1 small Spanish onion, medium diced
1 tablespoon minced garlic
1 teaspoon fresh dill
1/2 teaspoon sea salt
Pinch of black pepper
1 tablespoon white wine
1 teaspoon fresh lemon juice
4 cups chopped frozen spinach
1 1/2 cups crumbled feta cheese
2 medium tomatoes, sliced

Rinse and drain the rice. Combine the rice with 1 3/4 cup water in a 4- or 5-quart pot with a fitted lid. Bring to a boil. Reduce heat to low, cover and cook until rice is tender, about 15 minutes. Fluff the rice with a fork and gently mix in the currants. Cover and set aside.

Heat the olive oil in a sauté pan over medium heat. Add the onion and garlic and sauté until onion is tender. Add the dill, salt, pepper, and white wine and sauté a few more minutes. Add the lemon juice and spinach and stir until well combined. Remove from heat and allow to cool. Toss in the feta cheese.

Lightly oil the baking dish. Cover the bottom of the dish with the rice mixture. Layer the spinach mixture over the rice. Cover the spinach mixture with the tomato slices.

Cover with foil and bake at 350 degrees until the casserole is heated through, 30 to 40 minutes. Serve garnished with extra feta cheese and a drizzle of extra-virgin olive oil, if desired.

baked winter squash with honey walnuts

Serves 4–6

3/4 cup walnuts
2 tablespoons honey
1 tablespoon Rapadura™ organic whole cane
    sugar (or other sugar)
2 tablespoons extra-virgin olive oil
6 cups hard winter squash (such as butternut,
    buttercup, or kabocha), peeled and cut into
    large cubes
Pinch of sea salt
1/2 teaspoon of cinnamon

Combine the walnuts with the honey and sugar and 1/2 tablespoon of the olive oil in a small bowl. Toss well and spread out on a lightly oiled baking sheet. Bake at 350 degrees, stirring occasionally, until the walnuts are toasted and glazed with honey, 8 to 10 minutes. Let cool completely.

Combine the squash, remaining 1 1/2 tablespoons of the olive oil, salt, and cinnamon in a large bowl and toss well. Place in a baking dish with 2 tablespoons of water and cover with a lid or foil. Bake at 375 degrees until squash is tender, 30 to 40 minutes. (Baking time will vary, depending on the type of squash and the size of the cubes.) Gently toss the squash and transfer to a serving bowl. Garnish with the honey walnuts.

red lentil soup

Serves 4–6

2 tablespoons sunflower oil
1 teaspoon brown mustard seeds
1 teaspoon cumin
1/2 teaspoon coriander
1/2 teaspoon turmeric
1 small Spanish onion, diced
1 tablespoon chopped garlic
1 small carrot, diced
1 medium tomato, diced
1 1/2 cups dry red lentils
7 cups vegetable stock or water
2 teaspoons sea salt
1 tablespoon fresh lemon juice

Heat the oil in a thick-bottomed soup pot over medium-high heat. Add the mustard seeds and stir until they begin to pop—this only takes a moment so be careful not to burn them. Add the cumin, coriander, and turmeric and sauté a few seconds. Add the onion and garlic and sauté for 5 minutes. Stir in carrot and tomato and sauté for a few more minutes.

Add the lentils and stock or water and bring to a boil. Reduce the heat to medium-low, cover and simmer gently until the lentils turn yellow and become slightly mushy, about 25 minutes. Add salt toward the end of the cooking. Stir in the lemon juice just before serving.

dinners

dinner with moroccan flair

**Moroccan Tempeh or Chicken with Lentils ▪ Roasted Long-Grain Rice
▪ Pomegranate-Pecan Green Beans ▪ Spiced Cream of Mushroom Soup**

*When nutritious lentils are slow-cooked with all-natural chicken and spices, the flavor pro-
file that develops is incredibly deep. The vegetarian version with superfood tempeh is itself
a tasty treat. Either way, this is a dish that is truly protein-packed. When accompanied
by our Roasted Long-Grain Rice, Pomegranate-Pecan Green Beans, and Spiced Cream of
Mushroom Soup, this meal qualifies as a feast.*

moroccan tempeh with lentils

Serves 4

1 8-ounce package tempeh, cut into 1-inch cubes
1 tablespoon wheat-free tamari
1 tablespoon brown rice vinegar
3 tablespoons grape seed or sunflower oil
1 small onion, diced
2 garlic cloves, minced
2 stalks celery, diced
2 small carrots, diced
2 tablespoons tomato paste
1/4 cup red or white wine
1 tablespoon zahtar (a Middle Eastern spice
    blend)
1 cup French lentils
1 teaspoon sea salt
1 teaspoon capers
5 1/2 cups water or vegetable broth
1 tablespoon extra-virgin olive oil

Preheat oven to 375 degrees. Toss tempeh with
the tamari and brown rice vinegar and let sit for
at least 20 minutes. Toss with 1 tablespoon of
the oil and transfer to a baking sheet. Bake for 15
minutes. Set aside.

Heat the remaining 2 tablespoons oil in a large
sauté pan or heavy-bottomed pot over medium
heat. Add the onion, garlic, celery, and carrots and
sauté until they are tender and start to brown, 8
to 10 minutes. Add the tomato paste and sauté a
few more minutes until it starts to brown. Add the
white wine and stir to release any browned bits
from the bottom of the pan. Add the zahtar, lentils,
and water or stock. Cover and simmer gently until
the lentils are soft, about 40 minutes. Add salt
and capers and simmer for 5 to 10 more minutes.
Toss in the baked tempeh. Serve hot, drizzled with
the olive oil.

moroccan chicken with lentils

Serves 4

2 each chicken thighs, legs, and wings
  (6 pieces total)
2 tablespoons grape seed or sunflower oil
1 teaspoon sea salt
Pinch of black pepper
2 garlic cloves, minced
1 small onion, diced
2 stalks celery, diced
2 small carrots, diced
2 tablespoons tomato paste
1 tablespoon zahtar
1/4 cup red or white wine
1 cup French lentils
1 teaspoon capers
5 1/2 cups water or vegetable or chicken stock
2 tablespoons extra-virgin olive oil

In a large braising pan, heat the grape seed or sunflower oil over high heat. Add the chicken pieces and sear for 1 minute on each side. Season with a pinch of sea salt and pepper. Remove chicken to a plate and set aside.

Add the garlic, onion, celery, and carrots to the same pan the chicken was cooked in. Sauté over medium heat (adding a little more oil if necessary) until the vegetables have softened, 8 to 10 minutes. Stir in the tomato paste and sauté a few more minutes. Return the chicken pieces to the pan and sprinkle in the zahtar. Sauté a few more minutes until chicken begins to stick to the bottom of the pan. Deglaze by splashing the wine into the pan and scraping any browned bits from the bottom. Add the lentils and water or stock. Cover and simmer on medium heat until the chicken is cooked through and the lentils are soft, about 40 minutes. Add salt and capers and simmer 5 to 10 minutes. Adjust the seasoning to taste with salt.

Note This recipe may be finished in a slow cooker or in the oven.

After adding the lentils and stock, transfer the mixture to a slow cooker and set on appropriate heat level to complete cooking in the time you desire.

Alternately, transfer the mixture to a Dutch oven (covered baking dish) and bake in a 225-degree oven for about 2 and a half hours until chicken becomes very tender.

Finish with salt and capers.

roasted long-grain rice

Serves 4

1 cup brown basmati rice
2 cups vegetable stock
1/2 teaspoon cumin seeds
Pinch of sea salt
1/2 bunch parsley, well-rinsed and chopped

Preheat oven to 350 degrees. Wash and drain the rice well.

Place the rice on a baking sheet and bake, stirring occasionally, until rice starts to brown, 10 to 12 minutes. Set aside.

Heat a small sauté pan over medium heat. Add the cumin seeds and sauté just until fragrant, about 30 seconds. Remove from pan.

Combine roasted rice, vegetable stock, toasted cumin seeds, and salt in a medium pot over high heat and bring to a boil. Reduce heat to medium-low, cover, and simmer until rice is tender and the stock is absorbed, about 15 minutes. Stir in the chopped parsley and serve hot.

pomegranate-pecan green beans

Serves 4

1 tablespoon grape seed or sunflower oil
3 cups trimmed green beans
Pinch of sea salt
1/2 teaspoon pomegranate molasses
1/4 cup pecans, toasted and chopped
1/4 cup pomegranate seeds*

Heat the oil in a large sauté pan over medium-high heat. Add the green beans and sauté until tender. Sprinkle with a pinch of salt. Toss in the pecans and pomegranate molasses. Serve hot, garnished with the pomegranate seeds.

*Cut a whole pomegranate in half and then break the halves apart into pieces. Remove the seeds with your fingers or a spoon.

spiced cream of mushroom soup

Serves 4

4 tablespoons unsalted butter or sunflower oil
1/4 cup all-purpose flour
2 tablespoons minced garlic
5 cups sliced mushrooms
1 teaspoon sea salt
1/2 teaspoon black pepper
Pinch of ground nutmeg
1/2 teaspoon paprika
1 tablespoon cumin seeds
2 cups whole milk
3 cups vegetable broth
1 cup heavy cream
Minced fresh chives (optional)

Make a roux by heating 3 tablespoons of the butter or oil in a large, heavy-bottomed soup pot over medium-low heat. Whisk in the flour and stir constantly until the roux is heated through without taking on much color, about 2 minutes.

The texture will be somewhat sandy. Transfer the roux to a bowl and set aside.

In the same pot, heat the remaining tablespoon of butter or oil over medium heat. Add the garlic and sauté until just starting to color. Add the mushrooms and sauté until mushrooms soften and start to color, about 4 minutes. Add the salt, pepper, nutmeg, paprika, and cumin seeds and continue to sauté for 3 minutes. Remove from the heat. Transfer one fourth of the mushroom mixture to a bowl and set aside.

Combine the milk and vegetable broth in a separate pot and bring to a simmer. Keep hot.

Return the pan with mushroom mixture to medium heat. Stir in the roux. Slowly add the heated milk mixture whisking vigorously to prevent lumps. Cook, stirring often until mixture has thickened.

Use an immersion blender to puree the soup right in the pot or transfer the mixture to a blender and puree until smooth. (Use caution while pureeing hot liquid; keep blades of an immersion blender submerged and if using a blender, work in batches, filling the blender jar only halfway and hold cloth over the lid while pureeing.) Return the puree to the pan and heat over medium heat. Add the reserved mushrooms and the heavy cream and stir constantly until soup is hot. Serve garnished with chives.

dinner italian classics

Butternut Squash Lasagna • Vegan Vegetable Lasagna • White Bean and Kale Soup • Marinara Sauce

Lasagna. What a wonderful treat. There are many great versions of this classic dish and if you've never tried it with winter squash, here is your chance. The combination of sweet squash and creamy béchamel sauce wins fans every time. If dairy is not your thing, our vegan roasted vegetable lasagna will surely satisfy. Either way, the White Bean and Kale Soup rounds out the meal nicely.

butternut squash lasagna

Makes one 9x13-inch casserole

filling
1 large butternut squash, peeled, seeded,
   and cut into medium dice
1 tablespoon extra-virgin olive oil
1 teaspoon cinnamon
1/2 teaspoon fennel seed
Pinch of sea salt
Pinch of black pepper
1 tablespoon fresh thyme leaves

béchamel sauce
4 cups whole milk
1/4 teaspoon nutmeg
3/4 teaspoon sea salt
Pinch of black pepper
3 1/2 tablespoons unsalted butter
5 tablespoons unbleached all-purpose flour

for assembly
1 10-ounce package lasagna noodles
1 1/2 cups shredded mozzarella cheese
1/2 cup grated Parmesan cheese

make the filling:
Combine the squash, oil, cinnamon, fennel, salt, and pepper in a large bowl and toss well. Transfer the squash to a baking sheet. Bake in a 350-degree oven until squash is soft, 18 to 20 minutes. Return the squash mixture to the bowl and stir in the thyme. Using a potato masher or fork, mash the squash well but leave some amount of chunkiness. Set aside.

make the béchamel:
Heat the milk on medium temperature with nutmeg, salt, and pepper until warm. In a separate small, thick-bottomed pan, melt the butter, being careful not to burn. Slowly whisk in the flour and sauté for a minute on low heat. Slowly whisk the warmed milk into the flour and butter mixture, making sure there are no lumps. Simmer on very low heat to ensure it does not burn while you are preparing to use it.

prepare the noodles:
Cook the lasagna noodles according to the package instructions. Cool slightly.

assemble and bake the lasagna:
In a 9x13-casserole dish, layer in béchamel sauce, then noodles, then the squash filling, and then the mozzarella cheese. Repeat the layers using remaining ingredients.

Pour the béchamel sauce on the top layer of noodles, spreading it to the edges. Sprinkle the Parmesan cheese evenly over the top. Cover with parchment paper and foil. Bake for 40 minutes in a 350-degree oven. Uncover and bake 5 minutes more. Let rest for 10 minutes and serve.

vegan vegetable lasagna

Makes one 9-inch casserole

filling
1 large Spanish onion, diced
4 to 8 large mushrooms, sliced
1 red bell pepper, diced
1 small eggplant, peeled and diced
1 small butternut squash, peeled and diced
4 cloves of garlic, minced
1/2 cup of extra-virgin olive oil
2 tablespoons of dried oregano
1 teaspoon of sea salt
1/4 teaspoon of black pepper

for assembly
1 10-ounce package of rice lasagna noodles
1/2 recipe Marinara Sauce (recipe follows)

Combine the filling ingredients in a large mixing bowl and toss well. Transfer to a large baking dish or pan. Roast, uncovered, in a 375-degree oven until vegetables are soft, 35 to 40 minutes.

Return the vegetables to the mixing bowl. Lightly mash the vegetables together with a potato masher or fork. Set aside.

prepare the noodles:
Cook the rice lasagna noodles according to the package instructions. Cool slightly.

assemble and bake the lasagna:
Lightly oil a 9x13-inch baking pan. Layer in 1/3 of the Marinara Sauce, 1/3 of the pasta, 1/2 of the filling, 1/3 of the pasta, 1/3 of the Marinara, the remaining filling, the remaining pasta, and end with remaining Marinara.

Cover with parchment paper, then a layer of foil. Bake in a 350-degree oven until thoroughly heated through, 35 to 40 minutes. Let rest at least 10 minutes before serving. Garnish with a sprinkle of fresh or dried oregano, or basil, if desired.

marinara sauce

Makes about 4 cups

2 tablespoons extra-virgin olive oil
1 large Spanish onion, small diced
4 cloves of garlic, minced
1/2 teaspoon dried basil
1/2 teaspoon dried oregano
1/2 teaspoon sea salt
4 cups canned, whole, peeled tomatoes
1/4 teaspoon chili flakes (optional)
2 tablespoons chopped fresh basil

Heat the oil in a thick-bottomed sauce pan over medium heat. Add the onion and garlic and sauté until onions start to soften. Add the dried basil, oregano, and salt and sauté for a few more minutes.

Add the tomatoes and chili flakes (if using) and simmer over medium-low heat for 45 minutes to 1 hour. Use an immersion blender to puree the sauce right in the pot or transfer the mixture to a blender and puree until smooth. (Use caution while pureeing hot liquid; keep blades of an immersion blender submerged; if using a blender, work in batches, filling the blender jar only halfway and hold cloth over the lid while pureeing.) Return the sauce to the pan and stir in the chopped fresh basil. Use as directed in the lasagna recipe.

Any unused portion can be refrigerated for up to 2 weeks, or frozen for several months.

white bean and kale soup

Serves 4

2 tablespoons extra-virgin olive oil
1/2 Spanish onion, small diced
1 tablespoon minced garlic
1 carrot, small diced
1 tablespoon fresh thyme leaves
1 tablespoon dried sage
1 teaspoon sea salt
Pinch of black pepper
8 cups vegetable stock
1 1/2 cups cooked cannellini beans or 1/2 cup
    dry beans*
2 cups chopped, stemmed kale

Heat the oil in a heavy-bottomed soup pot over medium-high heat. Add the onion, garlic, and carrot and sauté for 5 minutes. Add the fresh thyme, dried sage, salt, and pepper and cook for a few more minutes. Add the vegetable stock and beans and bring to a boil. Reduce heat to medium and simmer for 20 minutes. Add the kale and simmer for 1 minute. Serve hot.

*If using dry beans, rinse and then soak overnight. Drain and place in a medium pan with 2 cups water and a 1-inch piece of kombu and bring to a boil. Reduce heat and simmer until tender, about 40 minutes, adding a pinch of salt toward the end.

dinner asian–new england fusion

Maple Ginger Chicken or Tofu · Carrot Parsnip Kinpira · Sweet Vegan Squash Soup · Squash Bisque

This is one of those fusion cuisine meals that highlights many favorite flavors. The Asian-influenced ginger and garlic pair beautifully with New England's finest maple syrup. The slight crunch of the kinpira-style vegetables complements the tenderness of the chicken or tofu. And the velvety smoothness of the squash soup—whichever way you prefer it—ties the meal together.

maple ginger chicken or tofu

Serves 4

1 pound boneless, skinless chicken breast or
   1 1/2 pounds firm tofu, cut into 4 portions
1/2 cup vegetable stock
1/2 cup white wine
1 teaspoon sea salt
2 teaspoons sesame oil
1 teaspoon minced garlic
1 tablespoon minced ginger
1 tablespoon tamari
1/2 cup maple syrup
2 teaspoons brown rice vinegar
2 teaspoons sesame seeds
2 tablespoons sliced scallions

Rinse chicken or tofu and pat dry. Place either in a bowl with the vegetable stock, white wine, and salt and marinate for at least 1 hour, turning occasionally.

Heat 1 teaspoon sesame oil in a sauté pan over medium-high heat. Sear the chicken (or tofu) until lightly browned, about 3 minutes on each side.

Place the chicken in a baking pan and bake in a 375-degree oven for 5 minutes. Remove from the oven and set aside. (It will not be cooked completely.) If using tofu, place in a baking pan and set aside.

Add the remaining 1 teaspoon of the sesame oil to the sauté pan and heat over medium heat. Add the garlic and ginger and sauté until fragrant, about 1 minute. Add the tamari, maple syrup, and vinegar and simmer until sauce starts to thicken.

Pour the sauce over the chicken or tofu on the baking pan and sprinkle with the sesame seeds. Bake in a 375-degree oven. The chicken should reach an internal temperature of 165 degrees and the tofu should be thoroughly heated through. Serve hot, garnished with the scallions.

carrot parsnip kinpira

Serves 2–4

2 tablespoons sesame oil
1 medium carrot, cut into matchsticks
1 medium parsnip, cut into matchsticks
Pinch of sea salt

Heat sesame oil in a thick-bottomed sauté pan over a medium-high heat. Add the carrot and stir to coat with oil. Sauté for 1 minute. Add the parsnip and salt and stir to coat with oil. Continue to sauté the vegetables until they are cooked through but still slightly firm. Serve hot.

sweet vegan squash soup

Serves 2–3

2 tablespoons Earth Balance™ (vegan spread)
1 small Spanish onion, medium diced
1 teaspoon cinnamon
3/4 teaspoon sea salt
4 cups butternut squash, peeled and cut
   into large cubes
4 cups vegetable stock
2 tablespoons maple syrup (optional)

Heat the Earth Balance in a large thick-bottomed soup pot over medium-high heat. Add the onion and sauté until it begins to brown, 3 to 5 minutes. Stir in the cinnamon and salt. Add the squash and sauté for 5 minutes. Add the stock and increase heat to high. Cover the pot and bring to a boil. Reduce heat to medium and simmer gently until the squash is soft, 15 to 20 minutes.

Use an immersion blender to puree the soup right in the pot or transfer the mixture to a blender and puree until smooth. (Use caution while pureeing hot liquid; keep blades of an immersion blender submerged and if using a blender, work in batches, filling the blender jar only halfway and hold cloth over the lid while pureeing.) If using maple syrup, add it to the squash while pureeing. Return the pureed soup to the pot and heat over medium heat, stirring constantly until hot. Serve hot.

squash bisque

Serves 2–3

2 tablespoons butter
1 small Spanish onion, medium diced
Pinch of ground nutmeg
1/2 teaspoon ground ginger
4 cups butternut squash, peeled and cut
   into large dice
1 tablespoon fresh thyme
1 teaspoon sea salt
2 cups vegetable stock
3/4 cup heavy cream

Heat butter in a heavy bottomed-soup pot over medium heat. Add the onion and sauté until translucent, 3 to 5 minutes. Stir in the nutmeg and ginger. Add the squash and cook, stirring often, for 5 minutes. Add the thyme, salt, and vegetable stock. Increase heat to high and bring to a boil. Reduce the heat to medium-low and simmer gently until squash is very soft, 15 to 20 minutes.

Use an immersion blender to puree the soup right in the pot or transfer the mixture to a blender and puree until very smooth. Add the heavy cream and puree until incorporated. (Use caution while pureeing hot liquid; keep blades of an immersion blender submerged and if using a blender, work in batches, filling the blender jar only halfway and hold cloth over the lid while pureeing.) Return the pureed soup to the pot and heat gently over low heat, stirring constantly until hot. Taste and adjust seasoning as desired. Serve hot. (Optional: Top with toasted pepitas or homemade croutons.)

dinner light and lemony

Tempeh or Sole with Capers and Lemon Butter ▪ Red Pepper Polenta ▪ Winter Ratatouille ▪ Italian Bread Salad

This simple yet delicious sole with lemon butter makes for a very popular dish, with the capers adding just the right amount of extra flavor. The tempeh version is so amazing you'll want to try it even if you are not traditionally a tempeh lover. Our Winter Ratatouille is perfect on top of the polenta. And though already a full meal, I couldn't resist offering you my favorite Italian Bread Salad recipe.

tempeh with capers and lemon butter

Serves 4

1/4 cup tamari
1 1/4 cups vegetable stock
3/4 cup dry white wine
2 8-ounce packages of tempeh
1 cup unbleached all-pupose flour
1/2 teaspoon sea salt
Pinch black pepper
4 tablespoons safflower oil
3 tablespoons extra-virgin olive oil
3 shallots, minced
2 cloves garlic, minced
3 tablespoons capers
1 cup white wine
1/2 cup vegetable stock
3 tablespoons Earth Balance™ (vegan spread)
Juice of 1 lemon
2 tablespoons finely chopped parsley

In a medium pot, combine tamari, vegetable stock, and wine and simmer over medium heat.

Cut each piece of tempeh diagonally into 12 thin slices. Place in the pot of broth and simmer gently for at least 30 minutes. Remove the tempeh and let cool.

Combine the flour, salt, and pepper in a shallow bowl. Add the cooled tempeh slices and coat each piece with flour mixture.

Heat the safflower oil in a large sauté pan over medium-high heat. Carefully place each piece of tempeh in the pan and brown on both sides. Transfer to an oven-proof serving dish and place in a low oven to keep warm.

Wipe the oil from the pan and add the olive oil. Heat over medium heat and add the garlic and shallots. Sauté for 3 minutes. Add the capers and sauté for 1 minute. Add the white wine and cook until it has reduced by half. Add the vegetable stock and cook until is has reduced by half. Stir in the Earth Balance, lemon juice, and parsley. Remove tempeh from oven and cover with sauce. Serve hot.

sole with capers and lemon butter

Serves 3

1 1/2 pounds sole fillet
1 tablespoon extra-virgin olive oil
Pinch of sea salt
Pinch of pepper
1 clove garlic, crushed
2 tablespoons white wine
3 tablespoons butter
Juice of 1 lemon
1 teaspoon chopped parsley
1 tablespoon capers

Preheat oven to 375 degrees.

Rinse the fish and pat dry. Rub with the oil and season with salt, pepper, and garlic. Gently roll sole fillets up, and place in a baking pan. Drizzle the fish with the wine and place in the oven. Bake uncovered for 10 minutes.

Heat 1 tablespoon of butter in small saucepan over medium-low heat. Add the lemon juice, parsley, and capers. Simmer for 1 minute, then remove from heat. Add the remaining 2 tablespoons of butter and swirl around until it is melted.

Place the fish on three serving plates and drizzle 1/3 of the butter sauce over each portion.

roasted red pepper polenta

Serves 4

1 red bell pepper
1 head garlic, rubbed with 1 teaspoon oil
1 cup cornmeal
1/2 teaspoon sea salt
Pinch of black pepper
1 tablespoon chopped basil

roast the red bell pepper and garlic:

Preheat oven to 425 degrees. Place the pepper and head of garlic on a baking tray and roast until the skin of the pepper is puffed and slightly charred and the garlic is soft and the papery skin becomes browned. Remove from oven and let cool slightly. Use tongs to transfer pepper and garlic to a medium bowl. Cover tightly with plastic wrap and let it steam and cool.

Separate the cloves of garlic and squeeze each one to release the roasted garlic. It will be soft. Measure out 1 tablespoon for this recipe and reserve the remaining for use in other recipes (or to just spread on bread).

Remove the skin from the roasted pepper and cut in half. Scrape out the seeds and membrane. Dice the pepper pieces finely and measure out half for this recipe. Reserve the remaining roasted pepper for use in other recipes or to spread on crostini.

make the polenta:

Combine the cornmeal, roasted garlic, salt, and pepper with 4 cups cold water in a heavy-bottomed pot. Turn the heat to high and bring to a boil, stirring often. Reduce heat to medium-low and simmer gently, stirring constantly until polenta is thickened, about 30 minutes. Polenta should be somewhat stiff. Stir in the roasted pepper and chopped basil. Serve hot.

winter ratatouille

Serves 4

1/2 large Spanish onion, diced
2 cloves garlic, diced
2 tablespoons extra-virgin olive oil
2 cups diced carrots
2 cups small cauliflower florets
1 cup diced celery
4 cups diced, peeled butternut squash
1 tablespoon tomato paste
2 tablespoons fresh thyme leaves or
    1 teaspoon dried
1 teaspoon dried tarragon
1 tablespoon fresh basil or 1 teaspoon dried
Pinch of allspice
1 teaspoon sea salt
2 cups canned, diced tomatoes

Heat oil in a large heavy-bottomed pot over medium heat. Add the onion and garlic and sauté until starting to brown, 5 to 8 minutes. Add the carrots and cauliflower and sauté 1 minute. Add celery and squash and sauté for a few minutes to coat with oil. Stir in the tomato paste and sauté a few more minutes. Stir in the thyme, tarragon, basil, allspice, and salt and sauté a few more minutes. Stir in the tomatoes and 1 cup of water. Cover and simmer until vegetables are tender, about 30 minutes. Serve over polenta—or whatever suits your fancy!

italian bread salad

Serves 4

for the dressing
1 clove garlic, minced
3 tablespoons extra-virgin olive oil
1 teaspoon balsamic vinegar
Pinch of sea salt
Pinch of black pepper (optional)

for the salad
1/2 loaf of your favorite Italian-style bread
1 tablespoon plus 1 teaspoon extra-virgin olive oil
Pinch of dried oregano
1 cup thick-sliced red onion
2 cups tomato wedges
1 cup chopped, peeled, and seeded cucumber
2 tablespoons sliced basil

Combine the dressing ingredients in a bowl and whisk together until well-combined. Set aside.

Cut bread into thick slices. Brush both sides with 1 tablespoon of the oil and sprinkle with oregano. Place on a baking sheet and bake until crispy, 6 to 7 minutes. Remove from the oven and let cool. Cut toasted bread into large cubes.

Heat the remaining 1 teaspoon oil in a sauté pan over high heat. Add the onion and sauté, stirring constantly, until it begins to soften but remain crispy. Remove from the heat and set aside to cool.

Combine the tomato wedges, cucumber, and sliced basil with the sautéed onion and dressing in a large bowl. Add the cubed bread and toss gently. Serve immediately to keep the bread crispy.

dinner seafood fiesta

Pan-Seared Shrimp or Tofu with Butternut Squash and Spicy Cilantro Pesto
• Coconut Lemongrass Soup • Roasted Quinoa and Corn

When our chef de cuisine Jeremy Smith brought me tastes of both his pan-seared shrimp and tofu dishes, I fell into a totally blissful state. Prepared either way, the combination here is a winner. The cilantro pesto is such a flavorful backdrop for the unique shrimp/tofu and squash medley. Over the quinoa the effect is perfect. And as if that wasn't enough, we pair it with the nurturing smoothness of Coconut Lemongrass Soup.

pan-seared shrimp or tofu with butternut squash and spicy cilantro pesto

Serves 4

2 cups small diced butternut squash, peeled
1 tablespoon extra-virgin olive oil
1 recipe Spicy Cilantro Pesto (recipe on next page)

shrimp version
1 pound jumbo shrimp* (16 to 20 per pound),
    peeled and deveined
Pinch of sea salt and black pepper
1 tablespoon grape seed oil

tofu version
1 1/2 pounds firm tofu
1/2 cup white wine
1/2 teaspoon sea salt
1 teaspoon lime juice
1 tablespoon extra-virgin olive oil

to prepare the shrimp:
Pat shrimp dry and lightly season with salt and pepper. Heat the oil in a medium-size sauté pan over high heat. Add the shrimp and sear until they turn pink and are cooked through, 1 1/2 to 2 minutes per side. Remove from pan and reserve.

to prepare the tofu:
Rinse tofu and pat dry. Cut into 1-inch cubes and place in a shallow pan.

Combine the wine, salt, and lime juice in a small pot and heat gently over medium heat. Pour over the tofu and let marinate for 1 hour. Drain the tofu before cooking.

Heat the oil in a medium-size sauté pan over high heat. Add the tofu cubes and sear until lightly browned, 2 to 3 minutes on each side. Remove from pan and reserve.

to finish the the dish:
Heat the 1 tablespoon of oil in a medium sauté pan over medium-high heat. Add the squash and sauté until it becomes tender and starts to caramelize, 6 to 7 minutes. Add the shrimp or tofu and cook, stirring gently until everything is just heated through, about 1 minute. Remove from the heat.

Add the Spicy Cilantro Pesto and gently toss until the mixture is well-coated. Serve immediately over Roasted Quinoa with Corn, if desired. (recipe follows)

*When purchasing shrimp it is important both environmentally and nutritionally to buy large shrimp (16–20) sourced in the United States. For more information on making environmentally sound seafood choices, visit www.seafoodwatch.com.

spicy cilantro pesto

Makes about 1 1/2 cups

2 cups fresh cilantro (leaves and stems)
1/4 cup toasted pumpkin seeds
1/2 cup extra-virgin olive oil
2 cloves garlic, crushed
1 tablespoon fresh lime juice
1/2 teaspoon sea salt
Pinch of chili flakes
1/4 cup grated Parmesan cheese (optional)

Combine all ingredients in the bowl of a food processor. Pulse until the mixture is finely pureed.

coconut lemongrass soup

Serves 4

3 1/2 cups vegetable stock
1 3/4 cups organic coconut milk
2 slices ginger root
1/2 teaspoon chili flakes
1 8-inch stalk fresh lemongrass
1 carrot, sliced
1 cup cauliflower florets
1 teaspoon sea salt
1 large mushroom, sliced
2 tablespoons lime juice
1/4 cup cilantro leaves
2 scallions, white and green parts, thinly sliced

Combine the vegetable stock, coconut milk, ginger, and chili flakes in a 4-quart soup pot over low heat.

Lightly pound the lemongrass stalk and add it to the soup pot. Heat the mixture gently, without boiling, and simmer about 20 minutes to release the lemongrass flavor.

Add the carrot, cauliflower, and salt and continue to cook on low until the vegetables are tender.

Remove the lemongrass and add the mushroom slices. Gently simmer a few more minutes. Add the lime juice and garnish with cilantro and scallions. Serve hot.

roasted quinoa with corn

Serves 4

2 tablespoons extra-virgin olive oil
2 tablespoons finely diced onion
1 cup quinoa, rinsed
1 3/4 cups vegetable stock or water
1 cup cherry tomatoes
1 cup fresh or frozen corn kernels
Pinch of sea salt and black pepper

Heat 1 tablespoon of the oil in a 4-quart sauce pot over medium heat. Add the onion and stir to coat with the oil. Stir in 2 tablespoons of water and cover with lid to steam cook until they are translucent.

Remove the lid and add the quinoa. Increase heat to medium-high and cook, stirring often, until the quinoa emits a nutty aroma, 3 to 4 minutes.

Add the vegetable stock or water and bring to boil. Reduce heat to low, cover, and gently simmer until the liquid is absorbed, about 12 minutes.

Heat oven to 375 degrees. Toss the cherry tomatoes and corn with the remaining 1 tablespoon oil. Place on a baking sheet and roast until tomatoes begin to pop open, about 8 minutes. Remove from oven and let cool slightly.

Fluff the quinoa and add the roasted tomatoes and corn. Season with salt and pepper and gently toss the mixture together.

dinner country goodness

Herb-Roasted Chicken ▪ **Country-Baked Tofu** ▪ **Wild Rice and Hazelnut Pilaf** ▪ **Savory Sautéed Apples**

Whether you choose the chicken or tofu entrée for this meal (or both!), you will love the classic down-home feel. And not only do they both make a great dinner, they are also wonderful as lunch sandwiches the next day. The pilaf makes a great rice salad, and if you have leftover apples, try them as a pancake topping. Really, this is many meals in one.

herb-roasted chicken

Serves 4

4 medium bone-in chicken breasts
1 cup white wine
4 cloves garlic, minced
1/2 cup extra-virgin olive oil, plus more for
    roasting
2 stems rosemary, leaves removed and chopped
1 lemon, thinly sliced
1 teaspoon fresh thyme leaves
1/2 teaspoon sea salt
Pinch of black pepper

Rinse the chicken pieces and pat dry. Place in a bowl.

Combine the wine, garlic, oil, and rosemary and pour over chicken. Marinate for least 2 hours.

Preheat oven to 400 degrees.

When ready to cook, remove the chicken pieces to a plate. Strain the garlic and rosemary from the marinade. Put half the garlic and rosemary on the bottom of a well-oiled baking pan and place the chicken on top. Tuck the lemon slices around, on, and under the chicken. Sprinkle the remaining garlic and rosemary over the chicken along with the thyme, salt, and pepper. Drizzle the chicken with a little olive oil.

Roast until the chicken is cooked through (until an internal temperature of 165 degrees is reached) and the skin is crispy and browned. It will take 30 to 35 minutes, depending on the size of the chicken pieces.

country-baked tofu

Serves 3–4

1 pound firm tofu

marinade
2 tablespoons wheat-free tamari
2 tablespoons white wine
1 tablespoon extra-virgin olive oil
Pinch of black pepper
1 cup water

breading
1 cup fine cornmeal
1 teaspoon dried tarragon
1 1/2 teaspoons dried thyme
1 1/2 teaspoons dried sage
Pinch of black pepper
1/2 teaspoon sea salt
1/3 cup nutritional yeast

Rinse tofu and pat dry. Slice into 8 to 10 pieces and place in a shallow dish.

Combine marinade ingredients in a small pot and heat gently over medium heat. Pour over the tofu slices and marinate at least 1 hour. (Or you can leave the marinade cold and use to marinate the tofu overnight in the refrigerator.)

Preheat oven to 375 degrees.

Combine the breading ingredients in a medium bowl. Remove the tofu from the marinade one piece at a time and lay them in the breading mixture. Coat both sides and place on a well-oiled baking sheet.

Bake the coated tofu until golden brown, 12 to 15 minutes, flipping the tofu halfway through the baking time. Be careful not to overcook as tofu will dry out.

wild rice and hazelnut pilaf

Serves 4

1/2 cup wild rice
1 cup long-grain brown rice
2 1/2 cups vegetable stock or water
Pinch of sea salt
1 1/2 cups sliced fresh fennel bulb
1 tablespoon extra-virgin olive oil
1/2 cup toasted hazelnuts, chopped
1/2 cup dried currants
1/4 cup chopped parsley

Rinse the rices and drain. Place in a medium sauce pan with the vegetable stock or water and the salt. Bring to a boil over high heat. Reduce heat to low, cover, and simmer until rice is tender and the liquid is evaporated, about 20 minutes.

Heat oven to 400 degrees.

Toss the fennel with the olive oil and a pinch of salt. Place on a baking sheet and roast until tender, about 15 minutes.

Fluff the rice and gently stir in the hazelnuts, currants, and roasted fennel. Season with a little salt and pepper, if desired. Garnish with the parsley.

savory sautéed apples

Serves 4 or more

3 crisp apples
2 tablespoons Earth Balance™ (vegan spread)
1 teaspoon cinnamon
Pinch of ground clove
Pinch of sea salt
1 teaspoon fresh thyme leaves

Core and peel apples and cut each one into 6 to 8 pieces.

Heat the Earth Balance in a sauté pan over medium heat. Add the cinnamon, clove, and salt and sauté a few seconds. Carefully place the apple pieces in the pan and stir to coat with the spices. Pour in 2 tablespoons of water. Cover and simmer gently until apples soften but maintain their shape. Sprinkle with thyme and serve hot or at room temperature.

nurturing pleasure and gratitude
Grace Jull, poet and educator

Pleasure and gratitude are two of the most important ingredients to add to any meal. One compelling option for exploring pleasure in the kitchen is to sensually appreciate the foods themselves. A wonderful practice is to focus on one sense each day, deepening your perception of sight, touch, hearing, scent, taste, and essence. Really look at the outrageous contours of that potato or the tiny speckles or great swaths of color on the apples. Notice the sounds as you slice, cut, or consume food. Discover the symphony of sweetness, sourness, or spiciness in your mouth.

Gratitude is the other extremely enriching ingredient. Especially in the fall and winter, when there's a chill in the air and food production goes into dormancy, the bounty we have to nourish our body, mind, and soul is truly astounding to remember. For inspiration and romance, read some of the "Odes" of Pablo Neruda—"Ode to Tomatoes"; "Ode to Maize"—a wonderful celebration of so many things that are mistaken as commonplace.

Gardening and buying local products invite a direct appreciation of what it takes to produce food. To hear a farmer or friend talk about the devotional act of babying seedlings, dancing with the elements, and finally bringing in a crop adds a profound dimension to appreciating the food that appears on our tables. The journey and hands that helped each item we eat—the olive oil, the grains, as well as our more locally produced goods—support us in living in yoga, in union, expanding the profound reality that the world truly is one family.

dinner hearty winter dinner

Turkey or Lentil Shepherd's Pie · Barley and Wheat Berry Pilaf · Vegan Gravy · Berkshire Blues Salad

What kind of winter would it be without a nice shepherd's pie? Our turkey version is a wonderfully simple take on the classic, while our lentil version is packed with vegetarian protein and loads of flavor. The vegan gravy is great on both, and sides of our Barley and Wheat Berry Pilaf and our blueberry and blue cheese salad are a brilliant combination of tastes. We use a wonderful local blue cheese called Berkshire Blue.

turkey shepherd's pie

Makes one 9x13-inch casserole; serves 4 or more

turkey filling
2 tablespoons extra-virgin olive oil
1 medium onion, diced
4 celery stalks, diced
1 tablespoon dried tarragon
1 tablespoon dried thyme
1 teaspoon sea salt
Pinch of black pepper
1 1/2 pounds ground turkey meat
3 cups frozen corn

potato topping
6 Yukon potatoes, peeled and large cubed
1 cup milk
3 tablespoons butter
2 cloves garlic
Pinch of sea salt

make the turkey filling:
Heat the oil a large sauté pan over medium heat. Add the onion and sauté until translucent, 5 to 8 minutes. Add celery and sauté for another 5 minutes. Stir in the thyme, tarragon, salt, and pepper. Stir in the ground turkey, breaking up any clumps and sauté until cooked through, 8 to 10 minutes. Add the corn and sauté until it is heated through. Transfer mixture to casserole dish and set aside.

make the potato topping:
Place potatoes in a medium pot and cover with water. Add a pinch of salt and bring to a boil. Cook until a fork slips through potatoes easily, 10 to 15 minutes. Drain potatoes and place in a large bowl. Set aside.

Heat the milk, butter, and garlic in a pot over medium heat. Simmer gently for 5 to 8 minutes until heated through and fragrant from the garlic. Remove garlic cloves and discard. Pour the heated milk over the potatoes. Use a potato masher to work in the milk and mash the potatoes until they are your desired consistency.

assemble and bake the pie:
Spread the mashed potato mixture over the turkey mixture in an even layer. Bake at 350 degrees until potatoes are golden brown on top, 30 to 35 minutes. (Optional: add an extra pat of butter to the top for the last 10 or so minutes of bake time.)

lentil shepherd's pie

Make one 9x13-inch casserole; serves 4 or more

lentil filling
2 tablespoons of Earth Balance™ (vegan spread)
1 large onion, diced
1 tablespoon minced garlic
2 medium carrots, diced
4 stalks celery, diced
2 cups corn kernels, fresh or frozen
1/4 teaspoon allspice
2 tablespoons fresh thyme leaves
1/2 cup chopped parsley
1 teaspoon sea salt
Pinch of black pepper
2 cups French lentils, rinsed
8 cups vegetable stock or water

potato topping
6 Yukon potatoes, peeled and large cubed
1/2 teaspoon sea salt
Pinch of black pepper
1 cup plain soy milk
2 tablespoons Earth Balance™ (vegan spread)
2 cloves garlic, lightly mashed

make the lentil filling:
Heat the Earth Balance in a large heavy-bottomed pot over medium heat. Add the onion and sauté until translucent, 5 to 8 minute. Add the garlic and carrots and sauté for 5 minutes. Add the celery, corn, allspice, thyme, parsley, salt, and pepper and sauté a few more minutes.

Add the lentils and 4 cups of stock (or water.) Cover and increase heat to medium-high. Gently simmer the lentils, stirring occasionally. Check the lentils frequently and add more stock as needed to keep lentils from drying out. Most likely you will use all 8 cups of stock but sometimes lentils can be sensitive or stubborn so it is best to add liquid a little at a time. Cook until lentils are soft with very little liquid left in the pot. Transfer to a 9x13-inch casserole pan and set aside.

make the potato topping:
Place potatoes in a medium pot and cover with water. Add salt and pepper and bring to a boil.

Cook until a fork slips through potatoes easily, 10 to 15 minutes. Drain potatoes and place in a large bowl. Set aside.

Heat the soy milk, Earth Balance, and garlic in a pot over medium heat. Simmer gently for 5 to 8 minutes until heated through and fragrant from the garlic. Remove garlic cloves and discard. Pour the heated soy milk over the potatoes. Use a potato masher to work in the milk and mash the potatoes until they are your desired consistency.

assemble and bake the pie:
Spread the mashed potato mixture over the lentils in an even layer. Bake at 350 degrees until potatoes are golden brown on top, 30 to 35 minutes.

barley and wheat berry pilaf

Serves 4

1 cup pearled barley
1/2 cup wheat berries
2 1/2 cups water or vegetable stock
2 tablespoons extra-virgin olive oil
1 small carrot, small diced
1 cup well-rinsed, finely chopped leeks
4 cups well-rinsed, finely chopped, stemmed kale
1/2 teaspoon sea salt
Pinch of black pepper

Rinse the barley and drain well. Place on a baking sheet and roast at 375 degrees, stirring occasionally, until it turns golden brown, about 10 minutes.

In a large saucepan, combine toasted barley and the wheat berries. Add the water or stock and bring to a boil. Reduce heat, cover, and simmer until grains are tender, about 15 minutes. Remove from heat; keep covered and set aside.

Heat the oil in a sauté pan over medium heat. Add the carrot and leeks and sauté until carrot is tender, 5 to 7 minutes. Add the kale, salt, and pepper and stir until kale is wilted. Combine the vegetable mixture with the barley-wheatberry mixture. Serve hot or warm.

vegan gravy

Makes about 3 cups

1 tablespoon extra-virgin olive oil
1 small onion, diced
2 teaspoons dried tarragon
2 teaspoons thyme
2 teaspoons dried sage
3 cups large mushrooms
1/4 cup nutritional yeast
1 teaspoon sea salt
1/4 teaspoon black pepper
8 cups vegetable stock or water
4 tablespoons Bragg Liquid Aminos™ (all-purpose seasoning) or tamari sauce
1/3 cup brown rice flour

Heat the oil in a saucepan over medium heat. Add the onion and sauté until translucent, 5 to 8 minutes. Stir in the tarragon, thyme, and sage. Stir in the mushrooms and nutritional yeast and continue to sauté a few more minutes. Stir in the salt, pepper, vegetable stock or water and simmer gently for 18 to 20 minutes. At the end of the cooking time, stir in the liquid aminos or tamari sauce.

Use an immersion blender to puree the gravy right in the pot or transfer the mixture to a blender and puree until smooth. (Use caution while pureeing hot liquid; keep blades of an immersion blender submerged and if using a blender, work in batches, filling the blender jar only halfway and hold cloth over the lid while pureeing.) Return the pureed gravy to the pot and bring to a simmer.

Combine the rice flour with just enough cold water to make a slurry. Slowly whisk it into the gravy and stir until it thickens to desired consistency.

berkshire blues salad

Serves 4

3/4 cup walnuts or almonds
2 tablespoons honey
1 tablespoon sugar
6 cups baby spinach
3/4 cup crumbled blue cheese
1/2 cup dried blueberries

Toss the nuts with the honey and sugar in a small bowl. Spread out on a lightly oiled baking sheet and place in a 350-degree oven. Bake, stirring occasionally, until the nuts are toasted and glazed with honey, 8 to 10 minutes. Let cool completely before adding to salad.

Toss together or arrange the spinach, blue cheese, blueberries, and honey nuts in a serving bowl. Serve with your favorite dressing on the side, or lightly toss with a little extra-virgin olive oil and balsamic vinegar.

desserts

delicious desserts

Vegan Carrot Cake with Cream Cheese Frosting · Chocolate Peanut Butter Energy Bars · Indian-Style Rice Pudding

From the talents of the Kripalu Bakery come these tasty treats. With the exception of the cream cheese frosting option for the carrot cake, each of these desserts are vegan, yummy, and versatile. Try the carrot cake recipe as carrot muffins and, chocked full of carrots, walnuts, and raisins, I say it counts as breakfast! The rice pudding is great warm or cold, and the chocolate bars make delightful holiday gifts. Have fun!

vegan carrot cake

Makes one 9x13 or 1 9-inch round cake

2 cups all-purpose flour
2 teaspoons cinnamon
2 teaspoons baking powder
1/2 teaspoon baking soda
1/2 teaspoon sea salt
3 cups shredded carrots
1 1/4 cups sugar
3/4 cup sunflower oil
1/2 cup orange juice
1 cup raisins
1 cup chopped walnuts
1 recipe Cream Cheese Frosting
    (recipe follows, optional)

Preheat oven to 350 degrees. Grease cake pan.

Combine the flour, cinnamon, baking powder, baking soda, and salt in a large mixing bowl. Stir in the carrots and mix until they are coated with the flour mixture. Stir in the sugar, oil, and orange juice and mix until just blended. Stir in the raisins and walnuts.

Pour batter into prepared pan and use a spatula to spread batter evenly.

Bake until the edges pull away from the pan and a toothpick comes out clean, 45 minutes to 1 hour. Cool for 10 minutes. Remove from pan and let cool completely on a wire rack. Frost with Cream Cheese Frosting, if desired.

cream cheese frosting

1/2 cup cream cheese, room-temperature
1/4 cup unsalted butter, room-temperature
1 to 2 tablespoons honey
1 teaspoon vanilla extract

Whip cream cheese and butter together in a food processor or by hand with a fork until smooth. Add the vanilla and honey and mix thoroughly. Use immediately to frost a cake or quick bread.

chocolate peanut butter energy bars

Makes one 9x13-inch pan

for the bars
2 1/4 cups smooth, unsweetened peanut butter
1 1/4 cups raw pumpkin seeds (pepitas)
1 cup chopped pecans
3/4 cup raw sunflower seeds
3/4 cup maple syrup
3/4 cup honey
2/3 cup raw quinoa
1/2 cup flaxseeds
1 teaspoon cardamom
1 teaspoon cinnamon

for the chocolate ganache
3 tablespoons Earth Balance™ (vegan spread)
1/2 cup soy milk
2/3 cup sugar
2 cups chocolate chips

Preheat oven to 350 degrees.

Combine all ingredients for the bars in a large mixing bowl and stir until well mixed. Spread into cake pan. Bake for 30 minutes. Batter will puff up and still be soft. Let cool completely in the pan.

When the bars have completely cooled, make the chocolate ganache:

Put the chocolate chips into a heat-safe bowl and set aside.

Combine the Earth Balance, soy milk, and sugar in a small saucepan over medium-high heat. Stir frequently until the mixture begins to boil. Pour over the chocolate chips. Stir slowly with a rubber spatula or a whisk until smooth.

Pour the melted chocolate mixture over the cooled bars, spreading it to the edges. Place in the refrigerator for 1 hour or until firm. Slice and serve.

indian-style rice pudding

Makes about 4 cups

1 1/2 cups cooked brown or basmati rice
2 cups coconut milk
2 tablespoons toasted slivered almonds
2 tablespoons raisins
2 to 3 tablespoons honey
1/2 teaspoon cardamom
1/4 teaspoon cinnamon
Splash of rosewater (optional)

Combine the rice and 1 cup of the coconut milk in a medium saucepan over medium-low heat. Bring to a simmer, stirring frequently. Add the almonds, raisins, honey, and spices and simmer gently for 10 to 12 minutes. Remove from heat and cool completely. Just before serving, stir in the remaining 1 cup of coconut milk and the rosewater, if using. Serve cold.

Note If you'd like to serve this pudding warm, add the remaining 1 cup of coconut milk toward the end of the simmering time and continue to simmer until completely warm. Serve immediately so that pudding does not become too thick.

corn chowder *page 20*

spiced cream of mushroom *page 35*

coconut lemongrass soup *page 49*

sweet vegan squash soup *page 42*

red lentil soup *page 30*

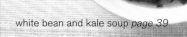

white bean and kale soup *page 39*

stocks and beans

stocks and beans

Guests often ask me to share the secret to our amazing soups, and I usually answer by saying it is a cook named Aggie. However, in addition to a heart-filled cook, the other key component to our delicious soups is in the use of stock. Whether you create a chicken stock or use a rich vegetable version as we do for most of our soups, a stock adds richness and depth. I recommend preparing your own stocks because many commercial stocks are loaded with sodium and they simply don't taste as fresh. And, if you utilize kombu, a sea vegetable, as we do in our vegetable stock, or a splash of cider vinegar, as we do in our chicken stock, you will find the flavor far surpasses that of any store-bought variety.

In addition to using stocks for all of the soups in this book, you can utilize stock in any recipe calling for water. Your pilafs and gravies will all benefit from the fuller flavor of stock instead of water.

Another key factor is the use of beans that we have cooked from their dry state. Be careful when buying canned beans. Although they are convenient, most brands contain a high amount of sodium. Also, most brands of canned beans do not utilize kombu. Kombu adds extra flavor because of its high mineral content and also helps beans become more digestible. Kombu is available at most natural-food stores. A little goes a long way and it can be stored for years. Use it in your stocks and bean cooking and benefit from the added flavor and nutrients.

And when cooking beans, try doubling the amount you intend to use in the recipe. This way you'll have extra to use later on salads or to add to soups or stir-fries.

chicken stock

Makes 8 cups

Bones of one chicken
10 cups water
1 teaspoon apple cider vinegar
1 teaspoon salt
2 cups mirepoix: diced onions, carrots, and celery
1 sachet of spices or bouquet garni (bay leaves, thyme, parsley, and garlic work well; for an Asian flare try garlic, ginger, lemongrass, and dried chilis)

Rinse the chicken bones and place in pot. Cover with water (make sure bones are covered by at least 2 inches), then add the vinegar. Slowly bring to a simmer but do not boil. Add salt. Allow to simmer 3 to 4 hours, skimming the top as needed. Prepare mirepoix and herb sachet and add at the 3- or 4-hour mark. Continue to simmer and skim for another hour. When finished, degrease if necessary and use or store.

vegetable stock

Makes 8 cups

2 tablespoons extra-virgin olive oil
4 cups vegetables or vegetable scraps (we suggest onions, celery, and a sweet vegetable like carrots or squash)
10 cups water
Sachet or Bouquet Garni of herbs and spices (bay leaf, thyme, black pepper, and garlic are favorites)
1 teaspoon salt

In a large pot, heat the oil and sauté the vegetables until they begin to sweat. Add water, herbs, and salt and simmer for 25 to 30 minutes. Skim impurities that float to the top. Strain and use or store.

cooking beans from scratch

Makes about 3 cups of beans

1 cup dry beans (any variety)
7 cups water
1-inch piece kombu
1/4 teaspoon salt

Dry beans must be soaked before cooking. The best method is to soak them overnight. Rinse beans first, then cover with 3 cups of water. Allow to soak at least 12 hours. Alternatively you can try the "quick soak" method. To do this, rinse the beans and place them in a pot with 3 cups of water. Bring to a boil and turn off immediately. Allow beans to sit in hot water for at least 1 hour.

Whichever method of soaking is used, discard water and place beans in a pot. Add 4 cups of water and the kombu. Bring to a boil and then lower to a simmer for 45 minutes or until beans are almost soft. Add the salt and continue to simmer until beans are cooked through, about 10 more minutes. Your beans are now ready to use. They will keep in the refrigerator for up to a week, or they can be frozen for extended storage.

index